WHAT GLUES US TOGETHER

Amethyst Garden (poetry)
Undertow of Silence (fiction)
The Unspoken of Our Days (poetry)

WHAT GLUES US TOGETHER

Poems by

Nancy Manning

Antrim House

Bloomfileld, Connecticut

Library of Congress Control Number: 2023900460

ISBN: 979-8-9865522-4-8

First Edition

Printed & bound by Ingram Content Group

Book design by Rennie McQuilkin

Front cover artwork by Sophie Greber

Author photograph by Cori Patchkofsky

Antrim House
860.217.0023
AntrimHouseBooks@gmail.com
www.AntrimHouseBooks.com
400 Seabury Dr., #5196, Bloomfield, CT 06002

To Mickey

Acknowledgments

Grateful acknowledgment to the editors of the following publications in which poems in this book first appeared, at times in earlier versions:

Craft Verses Inspiration, edited by Tony Fusco, Flying Horse Press, 2019: "September Tomatoes"

Noctua Review, 2022: "Exploration of Sheep's Head Way, Ireland"

Humans of the World (posting): "To Those Watching and Listening"

I thank my family and friends for the roles they've played in my life during my MFA journey and always.

A profound thank-you to my husband David and our daughter Kathleen. Their love and support have meant everything to me.

I am grateful to my siblings for having faith in me; to the late Harold Robinson, whose encouragement as a high school teacher inspired and led me to pursue poetic aspirations; to poet Nancy Naomi Carlson for continued encouragement; to the Hamden Poetry Group, my Women's Poetry Group, and my New Haven Poetry Group for their many suggestions.

Special thanks to my MFA professors—Jeff Mock, Pat Mottola, Tim Parrish, and Rachel Furey—for many critiques and words of wisdom about writing; and to the many MFA students, who offered their own helpful critiques as well.

Finally, a very special thank-you to my MFA professor and thesis adviser, Dr. Vivian Shipley. Her guidance and friendship through the years have made a profound difference in my life. I can't thank her enough.

Table of Contents

I.

First Love / 5
Birthday Wishes / 7
Muse / 8
Patient as Penelope / 10

II.

Anata Bakari / 13
Anniversary / 14
Masterpiece / 16
Thoreau Was Right / 17
Exploration of Sheep's Head Way, Ireland / 18

III.

Lost, Found / 21
Mickey / 22
"Writer, avid skier and hiker leaves family" / 23
One Tough Kid / 25
Turning Point / 27
Visiting the Institute / 29
The Walls Crumble Around You / 30

IV.

To Those Watching and Listening / 33
First Days / 34

Godless in This War / 36
September Tomatoes / 38
The Crash / 39
Family Meeting / 40
Granite State Goodbyes / 41
Our Own Walden / 43
Holding On, October 2020 / 44
At St. Joseph's Oratory, Montreal / 45
My Birthday During Covid / 47
Crocus / 49

About the Author / 51
About the Book / 52

*Leaning into the afternoons I cast my sad nets
towards your oceanic eyes.*

—Pablo Neruda

WHAT GLUES US TOGETHER

I.

First Love

Back in high school,
I followed you around like a lost
lamb, hoping you would shepherd me
into your life.
         Across Study Hall, we would catch
each other's eyes, but you always looked away.
At Mass I would sit in the alcove opposite
yours. If only we were sitting together,
holding hands.
         You were an Adonis among athletes,
dark-haired, dark-eyed. I dreamed
every soccer ball you booted
into the net, each basket you swished
through the hoop, all the baseball hits
you accumulated were dedicated
to me.
     After every tennis win I earned, I
pointed my racket in your direction.

I joined Model UN, but you had
already left. Became a CYO member,
but you started working at the pharmacy.
Many times I showed up, bought cough drops
and gum though you weren't running the register.

I wanted to read you my "Secret Sharer" essay,
recite for you a Shakespearean sonnet, but you didn't
linger long at your locker.

               During your senior assembly,
I was recognized for winning the poetry contest;
you didn't turn your head.
                    Through hours of the *Deer Hunter*,
I sat in front of you, next to my brother, waited for
you to tap my shoulder, ask whom I was with. When I turned
during the credits, you were holding another's hand.

On your last day of classes, I asked you
to sign my yearbook. You said, *You're a junior, right?*

Graduation night was the last time I'd see you.
You headed off to MIT, left me alone
in a small town I couldn't wait to leave.

Birthday Wishes

We were two college kids
in ripped jeans and Save-the-Earth
tee shirts. Poets by design.

You radiated, opening your gift—
John Updike's *Hugging the Shore*,
which I had saved up to buy.

I wished I was your shoreline:
your arms could explore me, wrap
around my lonely sand; your hands
could trace the contours of my rocks,
fill in gaps with your salt water. Your fingers
could comb seaweed curls of my hair.
Your tongue could soften the polish
of my driftwood. Make me more briny.

I waited the winter, each day
greeted the mailman,
stepped away empty-handed—
kicked through the snow.
Blew out another candle.

Later I learned you had moored
elsewhere,

      found a better beach.

Muse

Once in high school, you held open
the door for me.

You in your football uniform. Me in my field
hockey jersey

and skirt. In the breath of this dream, I hungered
for more.

Months later you visited my campus. Near the corner

arch we sat. You didn't like edges, points meeting. People
were parallel not perpendicular.

You wrote poetry, but never shared a page. Still your voice
floated

in rings around my head and your hands sculpted me. Like
Falconet's Pygmalion,

you crouched, looked adoringly at your Galatea of baroque
ivory—

hair braided, eyes beholden, mouth smiling. Breasts round
like white rosettes.

Arms and legs shapely. Abdomen beckoning life. You
breathed life

into me. We went to movies, walked around Walden,
watched football games.

Our hands joined, but our ideas didn't dovetail.

Years later, when I learned of your gunshot
wound, I broke into pieces.

Details of your death couldn't be shared.
Family prodded the shards

for answers. Tears flooded my cheeks.
Today, questions sill linger.

Maybe in death you glue me
together.

Blow away dust so
words

on paper exhale
meaning.

Patient as Penelope

Sunflowers lower their eyes. October
leaves kneel before their winter god.

We lounge on blanket, eat cheese
and biscuits, sip chamomile tea.

You read from Fitzie's *Tycoon*
and Ernie's *First Forty-Nine*.
I translate *Le Petit Prince*.

The sun winks good-bye. You tell
me you'll be away through spring.

Promise to return. A hand desires
a silken glove.

In the morning I find no more crowns
of violet encircling my head. Ink
on paper through distant miles

whispers my hellos. You reply in flat swirls
we were too young. Your heart

didn't flutter. Still I wait as Aeolus
keeps

     you off course on some ship
        docked in some distant harbor.

II.

Anata Bakari

(my one and only)

here where candles kiss
the night, I lie folded in your arms

for your heart is my heart.
our legs like stems, our arms like petals,

we sleep like the morning glory
that closes eyes to the dark,

awakens when the sun stretches
across the seascape sky and waves

lean forward, brush the shore.
We two bloom together.

Anniversary

Framed in white sandalwood, these watercolors
in pastel hues remain centered on our bedroom wall—
two Jill Walker sketches my husband and I purchased
in Antigua on our honeymoon over thirty years ago.

The first, *Golden Grove*, captures a domestic scene
outside a Caribbean home. Clothes flap on a line
tied between palm trees that flutter in a tropical breeze.
Free range chickens roam the yard, peck at seed
a young girl in pink leans over to offer. A man gathers
stalks of sugarcane near the white outhouse.
Four children play, one with his dog. A game of fetch
the stick. An elderly woman sits on a log, sips
from her mug. The mother in blue bends to collect
vegetables from the front yard garden. Purple
mountains grace the background. A blue sky alive,
lazy with clouds. Bliss after all these years.

The second painting, *Fishing Boats*, features four boats
moored in St. John's harbor. Each with a single mast.
Fishermen load their boats with supplies in cloth sacks
piled on their heads. The "Texas house" filled
with coffee, nets. Baskets are ready, a cooler filled.
Two seagulls soar in low swoops this early morning.
The sky dreamy with puffy clouds, the hint of a shower.
A tourism ship in the distance prepares to dock.
Fluorescent green the sea—these tranquil waters
invite another day's adventure, looming on the horizon.

Today, our anniversary, we lift champagne glasses.
Cheer that we have known domestic days—
snug in a bungalow, we cherish each day
with our daughter. Sailing away on other adventures—
back to the Caribbean or overseas to Ireland
or wherever our compass needle settles next.

Masterpiece

A rare photograph without my daughter, aged one.
In her place, a rickety clothes rack for winter drying—

tee-shirts, kitchen towels, bath towels underneath,
her bib and a cloth diaper on each side.

In the center, two rows of baby socks, six pairs
of them—lacy, white—represent her presence,

create symmetry, fill spaces that had been empty
more than a dozen years while I awaited her arrival.

Other photos show us reading Dr. Seuss,
hopscotching on kitchen tiles, sorting objects—

her brown eyes sparkling like beads she has tossed
into cups. To make music, she clangs pans.

Now she plays piano, flute, oboe, bass guitar.
I still have her baby shoes, a white pair

with scuff marks. Like these photos, they deserve
gold framing as they whisper of the past

as we ready for graduation, what will come next.

Thoreau Was Right

Here in my husband's Ireland,
wildness *is the preservation of the world.*
Hiking Sheep's Head Way,
          I meander through soggy ground,

climb over stone, trip over deep roots,
discover ruins of an old farmhouse—
a skeleton created by time.
          Collapsed roof and support beams pile

inward like crushed ribs. The limestone
chimney, pounded by wind, remains upright.
Even without a door or curtains, this house
                    has a soul. I imagine family

huddled before fire, sharing tales
of how Michael Collins fought to free this land.
Behind the house, into a shaded bower, I step.
                    Woodbine embraces the holly.

Fiery torches of red montbretia light
my way. I hear the shrill of a songbird.
Delighted by blackberries, I pick dozens,
          chew as juice dribbles down my chin.

Seagulls gawk. To the west, cliffs impose
their presence. Boats sprinkle the bay as fishermen
pull nets, smile upon the day. All this my husband
               left behind. My dream is to stay.

Exploration of Sheep's Head Way, Ireland

Pondering whether I am island or inlet,
   if the soul is external and the earth hollow,
   I find myself lost the third time on this trail.

Through low-lying cloud that kisses ground,
   I am caught in the clutter of fern,
   see only green. No one is around.

Deeper and deeper, my legs are swallowed
   as I am sucked down in bog, made to fall.
   Somehow I stand, learn to balance, free

my limbs, backtrack to shore. Relocate
   the trail for hikers and continue on.
   Now before me a bleached carcass of skull

and ribs and spine, spit back from the sea.
   I discover a cave, dark and inviting.
   A hidden home for Druids maybe.

A mouth of rock. My momentary shelter
   from rain and wind. The walls damp,
   I need a flashlight to see. An early explorer

may have sheltered here. Heard a banshee
   wail. Two seabirds coast overhead, remind
   me I have returned to this island to renew

a love of land, people. I reattach my tether
   to the world. Put pen back on paper. Continue
   building foundations under my dreams.

III.

Lost, Found

*To my friend Joanne Niland, in memory
of her beloved son Sean, 1993-2020*

Had it been returned, rightfully stored,
this old bucket would be a pail for milking

or sandbox play. Your son spent hours
at the beach, filling his pail then turning it

upside down to form mounds and mounds
of sand and ocean to be sculpted into castle

spires by his patient hands. Inverted, his pail
became a bongo drum he beat upon

or a snare drum he tapped with a stick.
His pail caught frogs he shared with his sister.

It helped scoop a bunny he brought home.
He lined the bottom with cotton balls

for the bunny's restful slumber. We nursed her
back to life with an eyedropper filled with

warm milk. A grin spread wide on his face.
But left out behind the barn, this old bucket

rusted, became less useful,
the moon and stars filling it with its only light.

Mickey

The first time I almost lost him,
I was five, sitting on the back porch.
He ran up the sidewalk, neighborhood
boys behind him. His face ashen as blood
spurted an angry fountain of red from his wrist.
He had been playing at the brook and fell—
a jagged piece of glass had slashed open his wrist,
sliced open the vein.
Mr. McConnell applied a tourniquet.
Daddy rushed him to the emergency room. Left home,
I kept repeating, "Don't take him. He's my *brother*."
I waited for hours for his return. Like the Savior,
the doctor performed a miracle, stitched him up.
The scar is still prominent now like an unwanted guest.

The second time he was almost taken from me
was last Christmas. Working at a nursing home,
he contracted Covid. The x-ray of his lungs
showed shadows where pneumonia clouded.
His breaths were asthmatic wheezes disrupted
by coughing fits. Fevers plagued him, night sweats
prevented sleep. Our sister Carol brought groceries,
homemade soup. I dropped off turkey dinner, portions
for five days—he finished them in two. Three times
he drove to the hospital, even during a snowstorm.
He was never admitted. Never given medicine.
Yet somehow we were gifted with another miracle.

"Writer, avid skier and hiker leaves family"

His obituary listed him as John Reardon Popkins,
but I knew him as "Jay." He married my friend
Becky, moved to West Hartford to teach.

We chatted for hours about CMT's and SAT's,
went to plays at UConn. He adjusted
his John Lennon glasses when he laughed.

He wove Beatles lyrics into lessons on poetry, fiction.
Pure artistry. Was summoned to the principal's office,
was told never to do that again.

They settled in Utah to ski and hike. When baby Catharine
died in her crib, part of him perished. He channeled
grief into stories, a novel. I loved every word.

I wish I had shared this story with him:

When I was ten, I nearly drowned.
Sun didn't penetrate the depths of Lake Marigold.

My body chilled when I lowered myself in. I was afraid
the waters would swallow me.

The lifeguard ordered me to swim from dock to dock.
When I didn't feel the floor under my feet,

I panicked, felt water pull me below. Down, down
my body sank though I flailed my arms, gasped to breathe.

My friend Linda saved me. Wrapped her arms around
me and kicked me to safety. I spit up blackness on the beach.

A lifeguard, Jay would have rescued me.

Last year on a visit to the Cape, he walked the beach alone,
watched the sun set. He emptied his prescription bottle, swallowed.
We couldn't save him; he couldn't save himself.

One Tough Kid

Hair short like a boy's, she challenged
anyone who gave her lip
though soft sketches wallpapered
her bedroom.

High school sports propelled her
into the spotlight. She was a three-sport
phenom. Her signature ponytail bounced
around as she sprinted upfield as halfback
for the Raiders' field hockey team.
She'd lean forward, jab her stick
to impede an opponent's progress. She'd steal
the ball, send it speeding to the center
for a quick score.

During basketball games, she wove
upcourt past others like Jerry West,
angled in a hook shot like Kareem
or slipped in an easy lay-up like Gail Goodrich.
She tallied insane stats by blocking shots.
We practiced this in the kitchen.
Despite our mother's warnings, she broke
the overhead light and cracked my ribs.

On the tennis court, she spun axles,
stretched to return an alley shot, aced
an opponent on her Billie Jean serve.
Why she was anchored in the three-doubles

slot, I never understood. The league awarded
her honors. Never have I seen a female
athlete mesmerize like her.

Turning Point

At college orientation, she turned heads. The only
girl majoring in earth science. Another science major
strolled past. Her life changed forever.

His blue eyes entranced her, set her heart
aflutter. It didn't take long to exchange numbers,
study together. Her junior year, he graduated,
so they married. But I noticed
cracks,
        gaps in their relationship where
differences   divided them.

He taught high school science and she
continued work toward her degree. At graduation
she was the pride of her department,
snagging honors for high grades.

Off to Miami, Ohio, the two of them headed
to earn Master degrees.
Tornadoes sent her
              reeling. Student
      cheating frustrated her.
        After   Father   died,
the pedestal of her weight
                didn't
                  seem
                    to
                      hold.

She returned home before the year ended.
Her husband transferred to Wesleyan.
She found work. Counted pennies,
reused tea bags, piled up dirty laundry.

One day she traced her husband's steps,
followed him inside the lab, discovered him
in another's arms. He denied what she saw.
Something inside her broke.

She tried to bleed him out of her self.
Was rushed to the ER—
to be pieced back together, stitched, made whole.

Visiting the Institute

I wait, vaulted in this room—walls white, bare.
Nothing but a table, four chairs.
You shuffle in, still wearing pajamas,
your hair pulled back, your face marred
by acne. An attendant by your side.

Your eyes keep scanning the room. Looking
for what? A clock? Some corner to hide?
I nod and your hands start to shake. You slide
them under the table. I wonder what meds
you have been prescribed.

Your doctors stitched you together but you speak
in fragments. *Fine. No. Kinda.* All sharp objects
have been removed.

My lips quiver. Your bedroom walls used to
feature your sketches of native Americans,
your fishing in New Brunswick, Canada, your hiking.
Trophies cluttered your shelves. How I wanted to be you.

You turn your head, say you're tired. It's time.
You don't smile, don't extend your arms.
Instead your hands shake more steadily
like Uncle John's. He suffered from Parkinson's,
never hugged us good-bye.

You reach into your pocket, pull out creased
paper. Your attendant leans closer.
You hand me a drawing, shaky stick figures—
you and me. Smiles beaming on our faces.

The Walls Crumble Around You

and the hole your feet are planted in
sinks you even deeper. Climbing to safety
isn't an option. You can't rescue
                      yourself.

You already tried to disappear into yourself
so pain would soften,
          but it didn't.

This time you ingest a handful of pills.
Curl up into a ball and wait,
like Daddy, who knelt alongside
our brown station wagon
and breathed in fumes.

But your roommate returns home
early. She calls 911, me—
implores me to help. The EMT's lift you
onto a stretcher,
          drive you away.

In the hospital, doctors pump
your stomach. Ask me your history.
Why would someone so beautiful,
someone so harmless,
          try to end it all?

IV.

To Those Watching and Listening

*Based on CNN Reporting: "Drone video team turns
the tables on hiding Russian vehicle"*

There was no staging what bombs have destroyed
in my grandparents' Ukraine. This Armageddon.
The ash thickens the air, settles deep in the lungs.

No one pretends to be a corpse shot or run over
by a tank, lies down on a road, and makes blood
pool on pavement. A person can't partially bury
himself in sand and claim, *See what they have done.*

There aren't enough coffins and body bags to empty
the streets. There aren't enough people to pull dead
from the rubble, bury, mark each grave.

Those who stay have no home, no heat, no food,
no water. Their days are numbered. They cry
before a camera and beg for these atrocities to end.

Drone footage captures how Z tanks hidden in forest aim, fire,
murder more innocent. How Russian soldiers drag away
the lifeless, loot them, discard bodies like unwanted trash.

First Days

Based on the Norman Rockwell
painting *The Problem We All Live With*

I remember day one of kindergarten—
my pixie hair, hand-me-down red dress
with a chipped button that my thumb nail
could not stop scratching.

I stepped outside my house, scuffed my black
suede shoes on the sidewalk as my stomach
tumbled with nerves. I missed the bus and had to enter
the classroom late. Pairs of eyes stared, made me lower

my head, so I wanted to disappear, never return.
My mother wouldn't stop apologizing.
If only I'd had the courage of Ruby Bridges.
Eight years earlier she had her own first day

in a New Orleans school, newly desegregated.
Her dress starched white, her braided hair accented
with a white ribbon. Young Ruby held her chin high,
feet in step with her smile, her ruler and primer loose

against her hip. Faceless but present, federal
marshals with yellow arm bands escorted
this six-year-old. An invisible army of white
women shouted, spewed venom.

These men couldn't protect Ruby from tomatoes,
racial slurs, obscenities that darken the canvas,
reveal generations of ugliness. Even today, hate
splatters blood on cement.

Godless in This War

Based on "Humid" by Joshua Eric Williams

Fragments
           of face, skulls
      of you—hollow
         eyes, slits
            of nostril,
blackened mouth—
                hurl at me,
Daphne, this laurel tree,
                  a tornado
of words—barbs
and
spears
      in a dynamo
           of wind
        that punches my trunk and branches.
Darkness,
only darkness
        as more blasts
      circulate around me,
        spin a dizziness,
                try to weaken
me,
topple me.

Your rage   explosive—
      I hear your suffering,
      wait for calm

and love

to return.   I am
woman protected.
Rooted,
deeply planted,
bark, stone,
leaves lovely jewels

you cannot steal.

September Tomatoes

Their scarlet skin shrieks for me to boil
them, squeeze them, strain their pulp

into sauce. Days of being on the counter
have swollen their cheeks into rage.

They threaten to sour. Like a sea of Cyclopses,
dozens of single eyes fix on me, demand

answers. Why would I, a gardener's wife,
postpone their fate? Picking cucumbers

can't be more important. One outcast
among them somehow rolls to the edge,

leaps to his death. I spring forward, make
a dazzling grab like a veteran third baseman

outstretched, just inside the foul line, body
parallel to the ground. Upright quickly,

I ignite a burner.

The Crash

Betrayed by glass, the goldfinch flies into my window.
A cluster of feathers—gray, green—explode,
float to the ground.

I run outside to save her. She lies motionless.
Her neck twisted to one side. Her beak pushed
into her head.

Gently my hands lift her. I find no nest, no babies.
I bury her in the backyard, mark the spot with a cross
of twigs I tie together.

Family Meeting

Around the table, we sit with straight backs.
You cower, keep your eyes unfocused—
your face twitches between words we utter.
When your doctor requests history,
the crooked smile slides off your face.

Mommy doesn't say a word, wants
this thunderstorm to go away, evaporate like rain.
My brother calls her out for being
unsupportive of his partner.

My middle sister rocks, remembers
Daddy's fist in her face, his hands strangling
her neck before he guzzled a beer.

My voice is firm, my list long.
I recount dates when my mother lost teeth,
when my brother heaved the kitchen table
so he could escape, when I stood my ground
and kicked my father's knee, when I intercepted
blows to protect others. So many bruises we bore.

My father stole so much from us.
All these years, my sister defended him.
This her doctor jots down.

Granite State Goodbyes

I didn't know when I said goodbye
to Lake Todd that August,
I was saying goodbye to you as well—
though you were well into your nineties.

My husband and I spent many summers
renting one of your cottages—a nest, brown
and snug in the woods.

Your fatherly attention warmed
my heart, filled a void that deepened
through the years after I'd lost my dad.

I dipped my daughter's toes
into patient waters on her first visit.
You held her like a grandfather and smiled.

We canoed out to Treasure Island,
observed the loons training their young.
I swam from my dock to yours as sunsets dazzled
the sky and we four toasted S'mores.

Souvenirs from around the world filled your cabin.
In the sitting room with paneled walls and lake
views, I sat at your feet, listened to stories
about your army days in Italy, skiing the Alps
to earn the rank of colonel. Just as you knew
your way around the Pentagon, you knew the best
nooks on the lake for fishing.

Before retiring, you headmastered a school,
disciplined with toughness—
though you gently asked me about my lessons,
what I thought of Conrad's "Secret Sharer."
You described playing the role of dissenting judge
in *Amistad*. You respected Stephen Spielberg.

But my favorite time was watching you
hammer cedar shingles, stitch a life preserver,
replace old dock boards, which reminded me
of studying the slow fingers of my own father
as he nailed sheetrock, snapped a chalk line
or twisted a socket into the wrench
and I'd hear the happy click.

Our Own Walden

For eighteen years, every April, my daughter
and I have sojourned here at Lake Sunapee.

To breathe, read, reconnect. Snow has cleared.
Ice has disappeared. Buds dot the trees; crocuses

and daffodils welcome us back as chipmunks
race by. We enjoy the healing hands of this lake.

Each summer we return—to hike, glide
on a playground slide, challenge the other

at the Adventure Park, paddle kayaks, lounge,
absorb the sun. We dine on the dinner boat,

enjoy the tour. But this month, I travel alone.
Silence invades my trip. Kathleen left the nest

well before I wished her gone. A lone mallard
paddles to my dock, welcomes us back.

Holding On, October 2020

Supplies of masks, test kits, beds, ventilators
are still hard to find as valuable minutes
tick away. Enclosed in my study,
I take time to think.

I list acts of kindness. Figure out to whom
I need to extend a bridge. My faults plentiful.
Too long I've gathered in worries. Raked
them into mounds

like fallen leaves, piled high that I'm too old
to jump on. Instead I need to dump them
in the back woods where they can decay.
Later be used as compost

for next year's garden. I'll shovel
a thick layer, work it in deep into the soil.
Try to cope through tough months that lie ahead.
We need to plough through winter. Await spring.

At St. Joseph's Oratory, Montreal

Up ninety-nine steps
I climb, my husband
by my side, telling me
to keep rising.

Twice every day
for three months.

We kneel on each step
of this marble shrine, recite
as one voice the Our Father,

and Hail Mary in a chant
that others understand

that I be cured
as Brother André healed
the boy, made him walk again.

Spring rain whips our backs.
Summer sun scorches our faces.

On the last climb, when we
reach the summit, I feel my
body cool, and I stagger.

My cancer has been silenced.
This baffles doctors.

If I had leg braces, a cane,
a pair of crutches, a wheelchair,
I would leave them behind,
add them to this expanding wall—

a testament of my cure,
proof of my recovery.

And each time my story is shared,
my husband and I grip hands
more tightly. Grateful that
we are alive, our faith has
intensified, like this tower of truth.

My Birthday, During Covid

Inside the 1754 House, comfort has replaced
rustic. Floorboards no longer creak. At a table
that doesn't rock, a young waitress hands me
a menu.

      Socially distanced, I sip my Merlot
as my eyes wander to the window, twelve over twelve
panes, and the view outside as cold air fights
to creep in.

      Across the street, an evening
performance entertains me. A spotlight at the Studio Hill
Gallery highlights a show unfamiliar to me.
      A wind
sculpture is set so that with each breath, Aeolus rearranges large
silver-looking lollipops atop a silver "T" bar.
      Then they become
twin unicycles seeming to balance on air, parallel. Turning,
twisting, these elements reshape as crossed tennis rackets.
Turning, twisting again
      they transform into a pair
of bubble blowers for children's hands. Turning, twisting
once more, they are scissors for a seamstress, and quickly now
chariot wheels for Ben Hur.
      Now a pair of magnifying glasses.
Elements revolving together, Dr. T. J. Eckleberg spectacles
view our pandemic world.

All the while,
yellow flames climb up the chimney, warm the room
as shadows dance on the white wall outside the gallery,
making me forget this Covid isolation.

Crocus

Despite winter, you manage it—
to burst forth from death.
Your corm, the onion bulb of your base,
opens and roots in frozen soil.
You push just enough earth aside,
stretch the bract of your body, as if
you have a soliloquy to deliver.
Snow melts in a halo around you, reveals
like a curtain pulled back, this solemn
act. Your long perianth tube flowers in six
purple petals, two whorls of three.
Stamen and stigma appear together. I smile
though the air chills. Year after year
you perform and I applaud.

ABOUT THE AUTHOR

Nancy Manning holds BA and MS degrees in English as well as an MFA in poetry from Southern Connecticut State University. Her work has appeared in an eclectic mix of publications, most recently *Humans of the World, Noctua Review,* and *Craft Verses Inspiration.* Her poetry collections are entitled *The Unspoken of Our Days* and *Amethyst Garden*; her novel *Undertow of Silence* won the TAG publishing award. She has given readings throughout New England. An avid reader, she participates in two book clubs and three writing workshops. She teaches high school English classes and lives in Oxford, Connecticut with her husband and daughter.

This book is set in Garamond Premier Pro, which had its genesis in 1988 when type-designer Robert Slimbach visited the Plantin-Moretus Museum in Antwerp, Belgium, to study its collection of Claude Garamond's metal punches and typefaces. During the fifteen hundreds, Garamond – a Parisian punch-cutter – produced a refined array of book types that combined an unprecedented degree of balance and elegance, for centuries standing as the pinnacle of beauty and practicality in type-founding. They were based on the handwriting of Angelo Vergecio, court librarian of the French king, Francis I. Slimbach has created a new interpretation based on Garamond's designs and on compatible italics cut by Robert Granjon, Garamond's contemporary.

Inscribed copies of this book can be ordered
from Nancy Manning
16 Oakwod Dr.
Oxford, CT 06478.
Please send $16 per book
plus $4 for shipping
by check payable to
Nancy Manning.

•

For more information on the work of Nancy Manning
visit www.antrimhousebooks.com/authors.html.
The author can be contacted at
nandanman@snet.net.